Your Gentle Support Companion

333
PERMISSION SLIPS FOR WRITERS
and other creatives

NATALYA ANDROSOVA

North Spirit Publishers
Toronto, Canada

Copyright © 2025 Natalya Androsova

All rights reserved. No part of this book may be reproduced, distributed, or used in any form or by any means, including photocopying, recording, or other electronic or mechanical methods, without the prior written permission of the publisher, except for the use of brief quotations embedded in critical reviews.

Editing by Amber Lambda
Book and Cover Design by Eswari Kamireddy

ISBN 978-1-7774537-7-0 (Paperback)
ISBN 978-1-7774537-8-7 (E-book)
ISBN 978-1-7774537-9-4 (Audio Book)

Also by Natalya Androsova

*15 Easy Ways to Overcome Writer's Block and
Start Writing Today*

*Dissertation Without Tears: How to Break Up With
Your Inner Critic and Nourish
the Writer Within*

*7 Minutes to Freedom: Simple Writing Meditations to Liberate
Your Writing and Your Life*

The Gratitude Effect,
Co-Author with Dr. John Demartini

Meet Natalya @ www.writingdissertationcoach.com

In this moment, you have everything
you need inside you
to flourish and thrive.

You just need to give yourself
permission to do so.

Acknowledgements

I am grateful to

Richard, for holding my dreams
in his heart with unwavering love and care

Angela Joosse, for her generosity
and friendship

Christina, for her kindness
and support

Amber Lambda, for being
clear and kind

My community of writer friends,
for giving me courage

My coaching clients, for being
inspiring and brave

Contents

Introduction   1

CHAPTER 1: Safety   8
CHAPTER 2: Explorations and Discoveries   12
CHAPTER 3: Joy and Fulfillment   16
CHAPTER 4: Curiosity   20
CHAPTER 5: Courage   24
CHAPTER 6: The Inner Critic   28
CHAPTER 7: The Writer Within   32
CHAPTER 8: Healthy and Sustainable Practice   36
CHAPTER 9: Pressures and Expectations   40
CHAPTER 10: Wrong Turns and Detours   44
CHAPTER 11: Resilience and Recovery   48
CHAPTER 12: Time and Energy   52
CHAPTER 13: Focus and Momentum   56
CHAPTER 14: Kindness and Self-Compassion   60
CHAPTER 15: Integrity and Self-Respect   64
CHAPTER 16: Self-Care and Balance   68
CHAPTER 17: Playfulness   72
CHAPTER 18: Self-Trust   76
CHAPTER 19: The "I Am" Anchor   80
CHAPTER 20: Clarity   84
CHAPTER 21: Faith   88
CHAPTER 22: Empowerment   92
CHAPTER 23: Freedom   96

CHAPTER 24: Wholeness	100
CHAPTER 25: Intuition	104
CHAPTER 26: Dreams	108
CHAPTER 27: Connection	112
CHAPTER 28: Responsibility	116
CHAPTER 29: Community	120
CHAPTER 30: Commitment	124
CHAPTER 31: Wonder	128
CHAPTER 32: Spirituality	132
CHAPTER 33: Gratitude	136
The Last Three Permission Slips	140
Three Special Bonuses	142
A Note From the Author	151

Introduction

Is this book for me?

Writing is mostly a solitary process. As writers, we spend a lot of time alone, one-on-one with our thoughts, our dreams, our doubts, and our inner critics. When we get stuck, frustrated, or overwhelmed, how we choose to talk to ourselves can change everything. It can support our writing process or crush our dreams.

I want this book to find you in moments of loneliness, confusion, despair, or overwhelm. I want it to be there for you when you're ready to quit and walk away from your dreams. I've been there. I almost walked away from my writing dreams so many times because I didn't know how to be my own friend and offer myself support and encouragement. I would love for this book to offer you a hand, giving you a new way to talk to yourself and a new way to support yourself and your writing journey. This new way starts by giving yourself permission to be who you are, feel what you feel, and do what's true for you.

I hope that by reading this book, you discover three companions who can always be there for you on your writing journey—freedom, acceptance, and self-compassion.

What if I'm not a writer?

You don't need to be a writer to benefit from this book because every creative process includes challenges and requires clarity, resilience, and strength. And every creative process can benefit from permissions to be authentic, courageous, and free.

I feel that, as creatives, we can learn to lean more on our strengths, values, and self-compassion when facing challenges. We can become not only productive, but unstoppable, joyful, and inspired. We can learn to savour every stage of the creative process because embracing all of them will help us acknowledge our strength and awareness. By not turning away from challenges, we can discover something infinitely more valuable and precious than any coping mechanism could ever offer us.

After each challenge we face and each discovery we make, we will be able to move forward more confidently, knowing that we can trust ourselves to get through any obstacle and recover from even the biggest setbacks.

Whether you're a writer or a painter, dancer, or film-maker, what I want for you is to freely give yourself permission to create from a place of courage and authenticity. I want this book to help you remove any pressures and expectations that you've put on yourself and build a healthy, sustainable practice.

Whichever art form you choose to create in, the world needs your unique vision and voice. I hope this little book gives you permission and encouragement to start creating today!

How one simple permission changed my life

Six years ago, I decided to write my first book. I'd published before as a ghost writer, but this was my first attempt to share my love of writing in my own book. I shared the draft with an editor whose work I admired and was ecstatic to move forward with a strong ally who would guide and support me.

Instead, I received very harsh feedback with lots of corrections and not a word of support. My whole world collapsed, burying all my writing dreams underneath the rubble. I felt crushed and unable to move. I was in shock. There was nothing wrong with my reaction. The trouble was, I remained frozen for three years, unable to touch my book. I was ready to walk away from my dream of sharing my heart with the world. I felt like an imposter. I gained a lot of weight. I stopped writing. I was ready to give up.

I shudder when I think I almost didn't publish the book. The initial crushing feedback from the editor was followed by years of rejections from literary agents. I felt defeated and paralysed. I decided that the book was worthless. And I felt pretty worthless too. I didn't know what to do. I surrendered my dream to my fear and crawled under an imaginary bed, like a little child. The world felt like too much.

One day, out of nowhere, a very quiet voice came from within and informed the scared little girl inside me that we were going to take a chance on our dream and self-publish. I didn't know where this voice came from, but in that moment, I felt a strange courage to trust it, and I knew there would be no going back.

It took me seven months to learn everything I could about self-publishing. I didn't have money to hire a hybrid publisher or a marketing team. I walked my journey by myself in the best way I knew how. One hard step after another. Into the unknown and into my fears. I gave myself permission to take a chance on my dream. I gave myself permission to be my own friend and supporter when I was trembling with fear. I gave myself permission to move forward

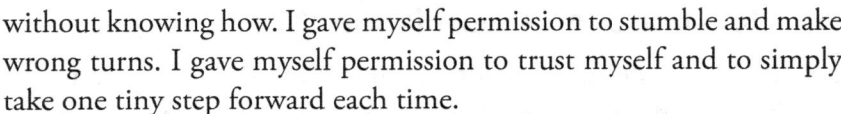

without knowing how. I gave myself permission to stumble and make wrong turns. I gave myself permission to trust myself and to simply take one tiny step forward each time.

When I finally published *7 Minutes to Freedom*, within days it reached the #1 New Release in 12 categories on Amazon in the United States and Canada. And in the Creativity category, I shared a spot right next to my idol, Julia Cameron, who had inspired my book and my entire writing life. I could never ask for more. I felt complete.

I wrote three more books in the four years since that time, and they all did very well, receiving mostly five-star reviews and reaching #1 in the New Release category in several countries. But this is not what matters. What matters is that my heart is full because I took a chance on my dreams and I am doing what I love. I did not betray myself or my dream. I have developed a loving relationship with my writer within and am supporting other writers on the same journey from self-doubt to self-trust through my coaching, workshops, and retreats.

In thousands of coaching conversations I've had with other writers and creatives, I've learned that it's often the same small permissions—to be ourselves, to follow our dreams, to use our authentic voices, and to enjoy our creative process—that have the power to take us from a breakdown to a breakthrough.

Never underestimate your own courage, resilience, and strength. You can support yourself and your dreams when no one else is there to support you. I'm here to tell you that you can turn any project you are currently dreaming of into reality. You have the power and the permission to do so.

May you lose the doubt and let your soul fly!

How to use this book

I chose 33 topics—such as courage, kindness, clarity, and inner critic—that can support or disrupt our creative process. Each topic became a chapter that starts with a brief reflection and then offers 10 permission slips for you to play with. I'm introducing the permissions in the order that makes sense to me, but you can move through them in any way that resonates with you the moment you pick up the book. At the end of the book, there are three bonus sections that invite you to apply what you've learned by offering you three writing challenges and questions for further growth.

This is a gentle writing support companion, and you choose what kind of support you need on any given day. Take what you need. You are in charge. And I am in your corner.

Each of our journeys is unique, but it seems that in the creative process, we tend to move in a similar direction—from entertaining the possibility of creating something to allowing ourselves the risk and excitement of actually preparing to take action. Finally, we trust ourselves to take a step and might even feel grateful for the opportunity to do so. So I organized the permissions in that order (example below).

You can try saying each permission out loud and pay close attention to the response in your body. Some days you will feel stronger and more grounded, able to move forward quickly. Other days you will feel more tender and will need to tread lightly, leaning more on self-compassion than on your goals. Please honour how you feel in that moment. Even though this may be challenged by your inner critic, it will strengthen your confidence and self-trust.

If a particular permission resonates, you can repeat it more than once. At the same time, if you read a permission that doesn't ring true for you, there's no need to force it. Choose another phrase a little closer to the top of the list, so that you feel comfortable and authentic saying it.

For example, if saying, "I am grateful to play, explore, and experiment" feels forced and untrue for you at the moment, you can start by saying, "It's possible for me to play, explore, and experiment," and maybe tomorrow you will feel comfortable saying, "It's safe for me to play, explore, and experiment," or maybe even "I am ready to play, explore, and experiment."

Let's practice right now. Say the phrases below out loud and choose where you want to settle on—which one rings most true today? Allow yourself to rest there. You can try again tomorrow. No pushing yourself, promise?

> It's possible for me to enjoy my writing (creative) process.
> It's safe for me to enjoy my writing process.
> I allow myself to enjoy my writing process.
> I am willing to enjoy my writing process.
> I am ready to enjoy my writing process.
> I am excited to enjoy my writing process.
> I can't wait to enjoy my writing process.
> I trust myself to enjoy my writing process.
> I am grateful to be enjoying my writing process.

And feel free to add or delete any words to make a permission yours. You've got this!

CHAPTER 1

SAFETY

Do you feel safe when you write? Does the blank page feel like a safe place when you come to visit? Do you feel safe to play and explore new and old ideas?

In the past, when I would try to write, thoughts and feelings of insecurity would come to the surface. I'd hear the voice of self-doubt in my head saying, "Is it good enough to share? Is it safe to share? Are people gonna laugh at me? Do I have anything important to say?" Because I didn't know what to do with these thoughts and feelings, to avoid the discomfort, I would just avoid writing altogether. Procrastination and writer's block promised a familiar comfort of avoidance.

The truth is, even in those moments of avoidance and procrastination, I intuited that there was a way to enjoy my writing process, even though I didn't know what exactly that way was yet. I desperately wanted to discover the courage required to face my uncomfortable feelings and keep writing. I wanted to feel safe while watching my messy words being born. I wanted to love and accept my words, my process, and myself amid all the imperfection.

I'm here to say that it's possible! We just need to learn ways to feel safe when we don't know all the answers yet, when we're still exploring and playing with our fragile ideas.

Wondering if it's safe to start dreaming about writing and sharing your words with others? Let's take a moment to settle deeply into the feeling of safety before we dive head first into creativity and play. Repeat after me:

1. It's possible for me to enjoy my creative process.
2. It's safe for me to make mistakes.
3. It's safe for me and my words to not be perfect.
4. It's safe to express myself authentically without worrying about people liking or disliking my words.
5. I allow myself to enjoy dreaming and to cherish my creative dreams.
6. I allow myself to feel good enough to love, create, and share.
7. I am willing to trust my gut, even if there's a chance I might be wrong.
8. I am willing to experience setbacks, get back up, and grieve before moving on.
9. I am ready to protect my time, attention, and energy and direct them to my writing dreams.
10. I am excited to play, explore, try something new, and change my mind the next day.

Now that you've read my affirmations about safety, take a moment to write down three of your own. You can start with any of the following phrases that resonate with you and continue in another notebook if you feel inspired:

It's possible to…
It's safe to…
I allow myself to…
I am willing to…
I am ready to…
I am excited to…
I can't wait to…
I trust myself to…
I am grateful to…

1. _____
   _____

2. _____
   _____

3. _____
   _____

CHAPTER 2

EXPLORATIONS AND DISCOVERIES

Do you write only what you know, or do you also enjoy writing to explore and discover new ideas and insights?

When I realized that writing had the power to take me on a discovery journey, everything about my writing process changed. I no longer experienced the pressure to say something smart or important. Instead, I followed writing to places unknown and went on adventures in my mind I couldn't have experienced in any other way.

The creative process is a beautiful exploration of both what we know and what we don't. It would be a shame for anyone to be robbed of this inspiring experience of writing without any pressure—just a sense of discovery and exploration. The mind always wants a plan because it doesn't have the courage to explore without knowing. But the heart has this courage, so we can trust our heart to lead us in this creative adventure.

We can come to the page as we are, start the journey into the unknown by putting pen to paper, and come away with gifts, insights, and discoveries that are ours to keep. Writing is a wonderful space for exploring our minds and hearts, and it's also a great companion for navigating places beyond our horizon.

You can trust it.

Ready to explore and make some discoveries today? I'm so glad to hear this! Need some courage? Let's get ready for our writing adventure together! Repeat after me:

11. It's safe for me to go on an adventure with my writer within so that we can explore freely and make discoveries together.
12. I allow myself to forget about the final outcome for now and to simply enjoy the creative process.
13. I allow myself to experiment with completely new approaches, connections, directions, and possibilities.
14. I am willing to focus on documenting my discoveries one moment at a time.
15. I am willing to go on a journey in my creative imagination and to honour my discoveries by putting them into messy words.
16. I am willing to not know what I am going to write and start anyway, because I trust my hand more than I trust my mind.
17. I am ready to discover hidden turns in the road and secret places in my mind and heart.
18. I can't wait to find new imperfect words to try to express my thoughts, feelings, connections, and insights in order to give my inner world a new life on paper.
19. I trust myself to enjoy and experiment with my first thoughts, my imperfect ideas, and to watch the magic of my creative mind in action.
20. I am grateful for the freedom to choose what I want to express today.

Now that you've read my affirmations about explorations and discoveries, take a moment to write down three of your own. You can start with any of the following phrases that resonate with you and continue in another notebook if you feel inspired:

It's possible to…
It's safe to…
I allow myself to…
I am willing to…
I am ready to…
I am excited to…
I can't wait to…
I trust myself to…
I am grateful to…

1. _____

_____

2. _____

_____

3. _____

_____

CHAPTER 3

JOY AND FULFILLMENT

When was the last time you felt joyful while you were writing? Not the moment when you finished your draft, but right when you started. The joy of writing is completely different from the joy of having written. It comes from the writing process itself, and not only from a sense of completion. There's nothing wrong with feeling happy after finishing a draft, as long as that particular joy doesn't distract us from the pure joy of putting words on paper.

One of the biggest obstacles to learning to write from joy was my assumption that writing was supposed to be hard, especially in school. I accepted this myth without questioning. And it was hard for a while. When my focus moved from experiencing writing as a playful, fulfilling activity to achieving a good grade (an external validation), that joy disappeared almost completely. Pressure took its place. Luckily, I remembered experiencing the joy of writing when I was younger. I could still feel the sense of play, flight, and creative flow I had felt before school taught me to associate writing with performance that will be evaluated. Once I remembered that writing could be dissociated from the pressure of performance and outcome, joy and fulfillment were right there waiting for me.

I allowed myself the pleasure of writing fast so that I could simply enjoy putting my thoughts on paper while bypassing my inner critic. I knew that I would enjoy wordsmithing at a later stage and use my discernment to make my second, third, and fourth drafts better. But in the moment of writing, I allowed myself to create space in my mind by emptying out all my thoughts and feelings onto the page. I learned to allow and welcome all of my words and sentences as they came out of my head onto paper: imperfect and beautiful!

I'm convinced that we can return to this sense of joy and fulfillment right now and cherish it for the rest of our lives. There will always be ups and downs on our writing journey, but we can let joy take care of them. They don't need to go away because this joy is larger than all the uncertainties and fears that come up. It can include and hug them all.

Want to feel more joy in your writing process right now? Great to hear! Let's take a moment to invite joy and fulfillment into this moment and discover and release what's in the way. Repeat after me:

21. It's possible for me to enjoy every moment of my writing process.
22. It's possible to feel joyful and fulfilled as I write.
23. It's safe to allow my words to flow directly from my heart onto the page and accept them wholeheartedly in all their imperfect beauty.
24. I allow myself to write with a sense of wholeness, fulfillment, and joy from the start.
25. I am willing to step into the unknown with a sense of wonder so I can discover what joy is waiting for me on the blank page.
26. I am willing to send my inner critic off in a hot air balloon for the next thirty minutes (or choose a duration that feels both safe and exciting for you), so that my writer within and I can play and experiment freely.
27. I am ready to enjoy my writing process.
28. I am excited to look for creative ways to enjoy every moment.
29. I can't wait to share my words with others for the joy of sharing, not for praise or approval.
30. I can't wait to fall in love with my writing and build a healthy, joyful, and fulfilling life-long relationship.

Now that you've read my affirmations about joy and fulfillment, take a moment to write down three of your own. You can start with any of the following phrases that resonate with you and continue in another notebook if you feel inspired:

It's possible to…
It's safe to…
I allow myself to…
I am willing to…
I am ready to…
I am excited to…
I can't wait to…
I trust myself to…
I am grateful to…

1. _____

2. _____

3. _____

CHAPTER 4

CURIOSITY

Are you curious about your own writing and all the possibilities for exploration it opens up? Or are you struggling to find the motivation to start? Does anxiety prevent you from writing before you have a complete plan?

For me, one of the biggest joys of writing is the opportunity and the invitation to follow my own curiosity into the unknown. It hasn't always been this way, but these days, when I come to a blank page, I feel excited because a new journey of discovery awaits me. I'm coming armed with pen and paper in the spirit of openness, curiosity, and trust.

This is one of writing's greatest gifts. I feel free to explore any direction that I'm curious about, look at any phenomenon, person, or event, and imagine any connection between ideas. I will take the time to evaluate and revise later, but for now, I am focusing on possibilities alone.

I'm here to say that it is fun and safe to not know in advance and instead get excited about the upcoming adventures and discoveries in the writing session. This way, our readers have a chance to join us on our honest journey into the unknown and witness every step of our creative voyage, peppered with moments of courage, clarity, and insight.

Are you willing to trust your curiosity and follow it to unknown places so you can receive the gifts of discovery and insight? Great. Repeat after me:

31. It's possible for me to temporarily suspend all judgment and quality expectations so I can lead with curiosity, try new things, and make my own observations and conclusions.
32. It's safe to not know exactly what I have to say and to find out in the process of writing.
33. I allow myself to learn something new and interesting from my practice today.
34. I am willing to meet myself on paper and face all the things I still don't know about myself with an open mind, curiosity, and desire to learn.
35. I am ready to find out how the world around me and the world inside me will meet on the page today and what new shape of harmony and balance will emerge from this meeting.
36. I am excited to discover new insights that my writing practice will offer me today.
37. I am excited to discover what I have to say and what beautiful creation will be expressed through my words today.
38. I can't wait to find out what direction my thoughts will go today, follow them, and record what I discover every step of the way, as precisely, freely, and poetically as I can.
39. I can't wait to start today's journey on a blank page and to see what the page will show me this time.
40. I trust myself to fully enjoy the mystery and adventure of the creative process.

Now that you've read my affirmations about curiosity, take a moment to write down three of your own. You can start with any of the following phrases that resonate with you and continue in another notebook if you feel inspired:

It's possible to…
It's safe to…
I allow myself to…
I am willing to…
I am ready to…
I am excited to…
I can't wait to…
I trust myself to…
I am grateful to…

1. _____

_____

2. _____

_____

3. _____

_____

CHAPTER 5

COURAGE

What does writing have to do with courage? For me—everything.

To be a writer takes a lot of courage. First of all, before I even start writing, I have to look at things honestly so that I can find my voice and my truth. I have to be honest with myself and acknowledge certain things I was not ready to see prior to writing.

So, first, writing insists that I find the courage to look at things that may be uncomfortable. After I discover my own meaning and insights, writing asks me for another kind of courage—the courage to share my discoveries with others in an authentic way that is unique to me. Finally comes another kind of courage—the courage to remain vulnerable and open to their feedback.

Thus, as writers, we must stand open and vulnerable, showing everyone our heart. We must be authentic and true to our vision. We might feel naked or imperfect, and yet, we have to share ourselves in trust that our readers are compassionate, empathetic people who will do their best to understand our words.

We are all unique and may not agree on everything, but the more perspectives we share, the richer our world becomes. We're all here for each other on this brave, creative journey of life in the spirit of trust and kindness. This is what I mean by courage.

Natalya Androsova

Do you want to cultivate the courage to use your authentic voice and share your innermost thoughts and feelings with the world? Repeat after me:

41. It's safe for me to look at the things within that scare me.
42. I allow myself the joy of sharing myself and my words with others, even if I'm not sure how they're going to react.
43. I allow myself the courage to embrace all my imperfections and write anyway.
44. I am willing to share my innermost thoughts and feelings with others.
45. I am ready to be free from worrying about other people's opinions.
46. I am ready to share my heart with the world.
47. I am excited to feel the courage to be authentic, true, and free from needing approval.
48. I can't wait to contribute my voice to the causes I care about.
49. I trust myself to keep writing and sharing regardless of the feedback.
50. I am grateful for the courage to be a writer and share my heart with the world.

Now that you've read my affirmations about courage, take a moment to write down three of your own. You can start with any of the following phrases that resonate with you and continue in another notebook if you feel inspired:

It's possible to…
It's safe to…
I allow myself to…
I am willing to…
I am ready to…
I am excited to…
I can't wait to…
I trust myself to…
I am grateful to…

1. _____
   _____

2. _____
   _____

3. _____
   _____

CHAPTER 6

THE INNER CRITIC

Are you tired of the loud voice of your inner critic? Do you feel like you've tried everything to make it go away, but nothing's worked so far? One of the biggest mistakes I made, as a writer, was thinking that listening to my inner critic was mandatory, when it was completely optional. Have you been there, too? The inner critic is diligently doing its job by trying to protect us from failure, embarrassment, and humiliation. This doesn't mean we should stop writing until it gets quiet. Its job is to criticize, and your job is to keep writing.

Trying to make it go away only makes it seem louder. The good news is, we don't have to worry about it going away. It has no power over us. But we do. The superpower we have is to focus all our energy and attention on our words, *while* our inner critic is saying negative things about us and our writing. We don't have to trust anything it has to say. Instead, we can choose to trust our beautiful writer within. Every negative word our inner critic says can be a beautiful reminder of our freedom to place our trust where we choose.

Have you tried creating a visual of your writing sanctuary where you're safe from your inner critic? If not, you can do it right now. Close your eyes and imagine a safe and inspiring space that's completely off-limits to your inner critic. Are you writing on a rock by the waterfall? In a cozy cabin with the sunlight playing with the green around you? In a cabana on a sandy beach?

Take two minutes to imagine and enjoy it. This place is yours alone, and no one can come in here without your permission because you have the key. When your inner critic shows up, you don't have to unlock the door. Let it stand outside the door and share its opinions. Every time you write, you can come here in your imagination and lock the door.

Want to stop listening to your inner critic? Want to see through its lies? I've got you. Repeat after me:

51. It's possible for me to enter my beautiful writing sanctuary and enjoy this time and space that is reserved for me and my writing dreams only.
52. I allow myself to leave my inner critic outside of my writing sanctuary so I can enjoy the sacred time with my writing.
53. I allow my inner critic to say anything it wants, but I am finally tuning in to what my writer within has to say.
54. I am willing to cherish and protect my writing dreams from anyone who is unable to offer their support or encouragement at the moment.
55. I am willing to tune out all other voices until I hear my own voice loud and clear.
56. I am ready to break up with my inner critic and not trust anything it has to say because it hasn't earned my trust in all these years.
57. I am excited to set my inner critic free and release it from its self-appointed role of criticizing me and my writing.
58. I am excited to keep writing, no matter how loud my inner critic gets.
59. I trust myself to break up with my inner critic so that I can fully experience the joy of writing.
60. I trust myself to support my creative process and nourish a beautiful relationship with my writer within!

Now that you've read my affirmations about my inner critic, take a moment to write down three of your own. You can start with any of the following phrases that resonate with you and continue in another notebook if you feel inspired:

It's possible to…
It's safe to…
I allow myself to…
I am willing to…
I am ready to…
I am excited to…
I can't wait to…
I trust myself to…
I am grateful to…

1. _____
   _____

2. _____
   _____

3. _____
   _____

CHAPTER 7

THE WRITER WITHIN

Do you have a relationship with your writer within? If not, would you like to?

Most of us haven't had a chance to meet our beautiful writer within because our inner critic has been too loud for us to notice this part of ourselves. The good news is that we can start now. We can make a conscious effort to spend time together with her (choose your own pronoun), get to know, understand, and support her. And she will support you in return.

This could be one of the best relationships you'll ever experience, but you have to take time and pay attention to her voice. It may be hard to notice at first because it's not loud and obnoxious like the voice of your inner critic. It's quiet and soft. She doesn't insist on her opinion, nor does she get loud—she patiently and gently invites you to explore the truth of your own heart.

One day, after decades of being in a committed relationship with my inner critic, I finally realized that this relationship was optional. So I changed my alliance and aligned myself with my writer within. I started writing to get to know my beautiful writer within and hear her voice. I started protecting her from any criticism as she grew stronger, developed her voice, and felt more confident. I started nourishing our relationship and remained a loyal friend to her.

And now my writer within knows that she is safe in my care. She knows that I am always there for her. And she also knows that I trust her to make clear and empowered decisions about my writing dreams because they matter to both of us. Together, we're here to safeguard and cultivate them.

Are you excited to meet, honour, and nourish your beautiful writer within? This is just wonderful to hear. Repeat after me:

61. I allow myself to be playful and enjoy every moment of my writing explorations and adventures.
62. I allow my writer within to play and enjoy the process.
63. I am willing to support myself, my process, and my writer within.
64. I am willing to support myself and my writer within through every challenge and in the face of any obstacles in the best way I know how.
65. I am ready to believe in my writing and honour my unique ways of thinking, being, dreaming, speaking, and writing.
66. I am excited to get to know my beautiful writer within and to support her at all times.
67. I am excited to align myself with my writer within and protect her from my inner critic for the next thirty minutes of writing (choose the duration of your writing sprint), so that we can enjoy this writing adventure together.
68. I can't wait to give my writer within a chance to play and experiment freely, without a care in the world.
69. I trust myself to take care of my writer within and to protect her in the face of any mean remarks from my inner critic.
70. I am grateful to know my writer within.

Now that you've read my affirmations about my writer within, take a moment to write down three of your own. You can start with any of the following phrases that resonate with you and continue in another notebook if you feel inspired:

It's possible to…
It's safe to…
I allow myself to…
I am willing to…
I am ready to…
I am excited to…
I can't wait to…
I trust myself to…
I am grateful to…

1. _____

2. _____

3. _____

CHAPTER 8

HEALTHY AND SUSTAINABLE PRACTICE

For decades, I prioritized my goals over my needs. Almost religiously, I pushed myself to work past my limits no matter how I was feeling physically or emotionally. My commitment was to meet my goals at any cost, so I habitually dismissed my basic needs until I would crash and feel complete burnout. I eventually got tired of always feeling tired and started asking myself what made writing so exhausting. I got intensely curious about the ways my habits enhanced or sabotaged my writing process

I wanted to rebuild my writing practice so it would support me instead of making me exhausted and unwell. And I decided to support my process by learning new healthy habits. I started keeping a list of my unhelpful habits, fears, and beliefs so that I could investigate and change each one. I also kept a list of things that worked well. I got excited to learn what I needed in order to feel well while writing, and I committed to doing everything I could. I wanted to build a new kind of practice.

I started paying attention to my mental, emotional, and physical states of being. When I noticed that I felt tired or depleted, I would intentionally pause and focus on changing my state through breathwork, meditation, movement, journaling, fresh air, or nourishing my body. I also scheduled frequent rest and recovery breaks and put them into my calendar until they became unshakeable habits. The longer I worked on any given day, the more breaks I would take. After we inhale, we have to exhale, and creating a sustainable rhythm in our work allows us to maintain a sense of clarity and motivation with ease.

Do you also want to build a healthy practice where you support your writing and, in turn, your writing gives you energy and enhances your wellbeing? You can start rebuilding by paying attention to your relationship with writing and how you can improve your daily routine. You can also notice when you push yourself past your limits and miss the signs of tiredness, hunger, or mental fog. You can set an intention to stop before you hit your limits and commit to being well while you write.

Are you ready to make rest, reset, recovery, and renewal an integral part of your writing practice so you can enjoy greater creativity and motivation? Great! Repeat after me:

71. It's possible to make an intentional change and move forward in a healthy way.
72. I allow myself to schedule frequent rest, recovery, and joy breaks.
73. I am willing to work with my natural rhythm, honour my energy levels, and take breaks so that I can create the best work possible.
74. I am willing to keep trying, experimenting, and learning from my practice.
75. I am ready to question every unhelpful thought that comes to sabotage my writing goals.
76. I am ready to create a realistic writing routine that effortlessly integrates with my current daily rhythm.
77. I am excited to keep a list of my common distractions so that I can be vigilant and enjoy a healthy momentum.
78. I can't wait to modify my daily schedule so that I can align my writing time with my best energy.
79. I trust myself to create a writing routine that supports me and my life.
80. I am grateful to keep discovering new healthy, playful, creative, and sustainable ways of working.

Now that you've read my affirmations about healthy and sustainable practice, take a moment to write down three of your own. You can start with any of the following phrases that resonate with you and continue in another notebook if you feel inspired:

It's possible to…
It's safe to…
I allow myself to…
I am willing to…
I am ready to…
I am excited to…
I can't wait to…
I trust myself to…
I am grateful to…

1. _____

2. _____

3. _____

CHAPTER 9

PRESSURES AND EXPECTATIONS

Do you know the specific pressures and expectations you put on yourself and your writing?

Most of us haven't stopped to identify these on paper, so their power has increased because they've been secretly affecting our experience of writing all this time. We don't know why we feel so stressed, anxious, or stuck when we try to write a few sentences.

The good news is we don't have to do any complex or sophisticated maneuvers to remove them. We just need to take a moment to look for them, identify them, and let them go.

Once I was able to identify and let go of specific expectations I had for my writing (see the permission slips below), I was finally able to start writing for fun—without any pressure. I became content with simply expressing my innermost thoughts and got hooked on feeling the joy of free self-expression. I realized that even if no one ever reads, approves of, or appreciates my writing, I do. And it matters to me. This is my voice and my truth, and to have them appreciated by others is nice, but not to the point where it becomes an expectation placed on myself.

Sometimes pressures and expectations can help us push through because they serve as external motivators, but only until we discover the joy of writing. Who needs external motivation when you're having so much fun and enjoying every moment of your liberated creative process?

Are you ready to let go of all the pressures and expectations you've put on yourself and your writing and to finally break free? Let's do this! Repeat after me:

81. It's possible for me to release my need to receive praise, positive feedback, or any comments at all for my writing.
82. It's safe to let go of my need for my writing to be impactful.
83. I allow my writing to be useless and wrong.
84. I am willing to let my work not sell, be liked, published or critically acclaimed.
85. I am willing to let my readers like, dislike, praise, criticize, misunderstand, misinterpret, or ignore my work.
86. I am ready to release all the pressures I have put on myself and my writing, so my writer within can fly free.
87. I am excited to release all my expectations so I can play freely, inhale deeply, and fill my heart with enthusiasm and courage.
88. I can't wait to let go of my need for my writing to matter to others.
89. I trust myself to let go of my need for my writing to make a difference.
90. I am grateful to let go of my need for my writing to be liked, bought, read, or understood.

Now that you've read my affirmations about pressures and expectations, take a moment to write down three of your own. You can start with any of the following phrases that resonate with you and continue in another notebook if you feel inspired:

It's possible to…
It's safe to…
I allow myself to…
I am willing to…
I am ready to…
I am excited to…
I can't wait to…
I trust myself to…
I am grateful to…

1. _____

2. _____

3. _____
   _____

CHAPTER 10

WRONG TURNS AND DETOURS

How do you speak to yourself when you realize that you've taken a wrong turn or missed one and need to turn around and correct the course? What about when this happens in your writing or thinking, and you realize that you need to revisit part of your draft and set a new direction? What do you say to yourself when you notice that you're going down the wrong path and need to rewrite or delete a whole section in your draft?

Most of us are willing to forgive other people's mistakes, but somehow, when it comes to our own journey, we expect nothing short of perfection and struggle to forgive ourselves if we missed a turn or found ourselves taking a detour.

What if, instead of being hard on ourselves when we realized a mistake happened, we could celebrate our discernment and our new clarity? What if we could praise ourselves for realizing our mistake and not continuing in the wrong direction?

Once I discovered that my mistakes accelerated my learning, I was excited to learn from every "wrong turn." I realized that there were no wrong turns. Just lessons I could integrate into my life and practice. Every time I took a detour, I would move forward equipped with a new insight and a deeper understanding that I wouldn't have discovered had I not taken the detour. I became grateful for the exhilaration of making a U-turn and for each fresh start.

Instead of blaming myself for making a mistake, I could finally appreciate the courage required to make the most of my wrong turns—no longer remaining stuck for fear of making more mistakes. I got excited to try out new ideas, connections, and paths and to learn by experimenting freely. Each new detour invites me to practice discernment and self-compassion until clarity returns.

Want to treat yourself with more kindness? Want to learn a new way of dealing with wrong turns and be able to accept every mistake you make as part of the learning process? Repeat after me:

91. It's safe to take wrong turns in my writing.
92. I allow myself to take detours in my writing to allow my thinking to expand in unexpected ways.
93. I allow myself to make mistakes so that I can learn new things.
94. I am willing to take wrong turns in my writing in order to experience the joy of being courageous.
95. I am ready to embrace each failure and thank it for a valuable lesson.
96. I am ready to support myself through every challenge with gentle and kind words of encouragement.
97. I am excited to experiment with new directions and learn from every wrong turn and detour.
98. I can't wait to try new things and celebrate the courage it takes to move forward in the face of uncertainty and fear.
99. I trust myself to find my way back to clarity after every wrong turn.
100. I am grateful to take wrong turns in my writing so that I can practice kindness and self-compassion.

Now that you've read my affirmations about wrong turns and detours, take a moment to write down three of your own. You can start with any of the following phrases that resonate with you and continue in another notebook if you feel inspired:

It's possible to…
It's safe to…
I allow myself to…
I am willing to…
I am ready to…
I am excited to…
I can't wait to…
I trust myself to…
I am grateful to…

1. _____

2. _____

3. _____

CHAPTER 11

RESILIENCE AND RECOVERY

Do you know anyone who hasn't experienced setbacks? Me neither. The setbacks are not the problem. It's what we do with them that makes the difference between moving forward and getting stuck. Life is full of surprises, and circumstances often change without notice. Instead of dwelling on the unexpected things we can't change, we would be wise to look for the fastest way to get up, dust ourselves off, and move forward. Any setback can be used for learning and growth. I promise!

How do we help ourselves up after we stumble and fall? I'm not sure about you, but for me, resilience has always started with acceptance, gratitude, and trust. These three support me through every challenge and every fall. I hope they serve you, too, and inspire you to find your own combination of qualities you need in order to move forward after a setback.

I am excited to accept full responsibility for my dreams and to take good care of them. I trust myself to bring them to fruition by taking small consistent actions that align with my values and vision. During a setback, I don't need to push myself by setting big goals. My goal can be to gently "touch" my project for a few minutes a day, like open a document, read a paragraph, or jot down two bullet points on a napkin. A setback is not a reflection of my ability, but it can be a reflection of my resilience. I love myself enough to allow myself to heal, and when I'm ready, to get up, dust myself off, and start walking in the direction of my dreams again.

It took me a long time to learn how to support myself after a big setback or an unexpected crisis. I started by not rushing my recovery process and taking the time I needed to honour the feelings that were asking for my attention. I hugged each one and stayed with them until I felt ready to take the next step. I stayed with myself as a friend would, attending to the pain and offering kindness and compassion instead of focusing on goals. I'm here for the long game, and I am committed to accepting every stage of the process and honouring myself through it all. The ups and downs are an inherent part of the journey. They are invitations to find our own kindness and power.

Wondering what's the best way to recover after a setback? Want to develop a kinder habit of acknowledging without judgment, resetting, and continuing with your writing? Great! Repeat after me:

101. It's possible to feel creative, capable, and clear again after a big setback.
102. It's safe for me to reset and start dreaming again after a setback, even a big one.
103. I allow myself to experience setbacks without labeling myself as a failure.
104. I am willing to gently and lovingly "touch" my project during a setback.
105. I am excited to practice resilience after a setback and focus on one tiny step I can take right now
106. I can't wait to reset every time I stumble, so that I can get back to the joy of writing!
107. I can't wait to feel creative, capable, resourceful, and whole again after a big setback.
108. I trust myself to be able to reset and find clarity, momentum, and joy again.
109. I trust myself to keep moving forward, no matter how small the steps.
110. I am grateful to be able to lean on my strengths, values, vision, and self-compassion to move through every challenge.

Now that you've read my affirmations about resilience and recovery, take a moment to write down three of your own. You can start with any of the following phrases that resonate with you and continue in another notebook if you feel inspired:

It's possible to…
It's safe to…
I allow myself to…
I am willing to…
I am ready to…
I am excited to…
I can't wait to…
I trust myself to…
I am grateful to…

1. _____
   _____

2. _____
   _____

3. _____
   _____

CHAPTER 12

TIME AND ENERGY

Where do your time and energy go? Do you feel an abundance of both? How much of each do you have to give to your writing? We can become aware of our limited resource of time, our unlimited resource of energy, and our expenditure habits. We can build new habits that better support our writing. After all, time is not a renewable resource. Energy is.

Putting a timeline on any creative process can create instant pressure. We can learn to not rush our writing. We have all the time we need to discover and articulate our own meaning and truth. We can do it with clarity, precision, and beauty. We don't need to rush until we are satisfied with our unique creation. Let's focus on savouring every moment of our process and the joy of discovery instead.

When I acknowledged that I was more interested in gaining insight and creating a deeper meaning than in typing a certain number of words by an arbitrary deadline, my energy relaxed. This didn't make me less productive. Just more relaxed and focused.

I have all the time I need to do my best each and every moment. I trust myself to take the time I need in order to express myself with joy and clarity. There is no deadline or competition. This is my dream, and I am excited to honour it.

My new superpower is to be able to write from a relaxed, joyful, and fulfilled state. I want to bring my best energy to my writing, so my readers can feel the ease and inspiration I'm feeling as I'm writing down my words. They can sense and align with my energy, my emotional state, and the rhythm of my breath. With my words, I am welcoming them into my creative soul.

Are you ready to develop a new relationship with time and energy and enjoy having both in abundance when you write? Want to bring your best energy to your writing every time? Great! Repeat after me:

111. It's safe for me to take all the time I need to explore, process, and experiment with my ideas.
112. It's safe for me to take a break from writing in order to rest and recover.
113. I allow myself the luxury of time.
114. I allow myself the luxury of not thinking about time and deadlines when I'm writing.
115. I am excited to fully relax without guilt when I am resting and recovering.
116. I am excited to never rush my writing again.
117. I trust myself to pause when I feel like my energy could use a reset.
118. I am excited to forget about deadlines for the duration of my writing sprint and instead focus on my energy.
119. I trust myself to not sacrifice this moment in the name of a future one, even if it offers great promise, like publication or acknowledgment.
120. I am grateful to cultivate clear and joyful energy and enjoy each moment of writing instead of working towards a deadline.

Now that you've read my affirmations about time and energy, take a moment to write down three of your own. You can start with any of the following phrases that resonate with you and continue in another notebook if you feel inspired:

It's possible to…
It's safe to…
I allow myself to…
I am willing to…
I am ready to…
I am excited to…
I can't wait to…
I trust myself to…
I am grateful to…

1. _____

2. _____

3. _____
   _____

CHAPTER 13

FOCUS AND MOMENTUM

Have you seen these two dance together? Then you have witnessed their beautiful harmony, balance, and interdependence. You probably also noticed that one of the biggest challenges we face as writers is achieving single focus and momentum. So many distractions are ready to interrupt our creative process if we let them. The trouble is we do let them. I plead guilty, too.

To create writing momentum, we need single focus. Once we achieve this, the flow becomes effortless and self-sustaining, and in turn, helps maintain the focus. But there is no way to invite that initial momentum, except by creating conditions where all our energy and attention are focused on one thing only—connecting with our writer within, listening quietly to what she has to offer today, and putting words on paper. No other tasks. No phones, no chores, no email.

We are the only ones who can prioritize our focus and momentum, but it takes courage and commitment. It also takes new habits. In my own practice, scheduling and safeguarding my writing time was a game changer. Also, documenting and cultivating my most productive habits made a big difference. I experimented with different routines, paid attention to what worked, kept a list of my best strategies, and repeated them every time I wrote.

I also kept track of my favourite interferences and time-wasters and consciously set them aside. Before each session, I would eliminate potential distractions (clear my desk, put away my phone, etc.) and let my loved ones know that this was my sacred time with my writing and my writer within. When I was writing my first book, there wasn't a spare room for me to write in, so I put up a curtain to create a little writing corner. If you have children, you can have them make a "SHHHH... mummy is writing!" sign and have them put it on your door or the back of your chair before you start writing, so they are invested in the game.

Do you want to create the best possible conditions to invite writing momentum? Are you ready to give your work undivided attention and single focus to experience flow and momentum? So glad you said yes. Repeat after me:

121. It's safe to set aside all other tasks and dive head first into my creative process.
122. I allow myself to go into my writing sanctuary, focus inward, and listen to my writer within without any distractions for the next 25 minutes (choose your time frame).
123. I am willing to set up all the necessary conditions in order to encourage and maintain my writing momentum with love, care, and ease.
124. I am willing to do everything within my power to support my creative focus.
125. I am ready to keep my practice free from distractions so I can enjoy the precious writing momentum for as long as possible.
126. I am excited to give my best energy, focus, and attention to my writing.
127. I am excited to leave my phone outside of my writing sanctuary and allow myself to be undisturbed and unreachable for the next two hours (choose what feels realistic and safe for you) so I can create and enjoy the writing momentum.
128. I can't wait to protect my writing time and eliminate all distractions so that I can focus.
129. I trust myself to schedule short periods of uninterrupted writing time and protect them with my life so I can sink deeper into my work.
130. I trust myself to keep my momentum going and move through any block by finding a tiny step forward and taking it with courage and curiosity.

Now that you've read my affirmations about focus and writing momentum, take a moment to write down three of your own. You can start with any of the following phrases that resonate with you and continue in another notebook if you feel inspired:

It's possible to…
It's safe to…
I allow myself to…
I am willing to…
I am ready to…
I am excited to…
I can't wait to…
I trust myself to…
I am grateful to…

1. _____
   _____

2. _____
   _____

3. _____
   _____

CHAPTER 14

KINDNESS AND SELF-COMPASSION

How much space do you leave for kindness and compassion in your practice?

As writers, we mostly focus on learning new writing strategies, improving our sentence structure, making our process more efficient and our word choice more precise.

But when these strategies stop working, and you feel stuck, lost, or overwhelmed, do you remain kind to yourself and your writing? Do you meet yourself in the moment with open arms, give yourself a hug and enough space to reset and restore your confidence? Or do you side with your inner critic and start berating yourself and demanding perfection, even if you're doing something for the first time?

I used to motivate myself with unkind words and push myself to meet unrealistic goals because I mistook the voice of my inner critic for my own. I thought it was the only way to get better. Once I met my writer within, I realized that wasn't the case. Turns out I can motivate myself much better with kind and gentle words of encouragement. So even though it took a bit of time to see through my inner critic's mean comments and set myself free, it was worth the effort and I've been enjoying writing without my inner critic ever since.

I've also learned that when I am kind and accepting of myself, even when I stumble and fall, my creativity awakens, my ideas start flowing, and my writer within thrives and creates from abundance and wholeness. I still honour my desire to succeed by focusing on the choices and actions within my power to move toward my goals. But after each fall, I feel empowered and enriched by the new lesson, and it encourages me to keep going until I reach my destination.

Are you ready to finally be kind to yourself and your writing? Want to see how much better your writing experience becomes when you do? Today and for the rest of your life. Let's dive in! Repeat after me:

131. It's safe to allow my words to come out crooked and sloppy, awkward and funny, nonsensical and childish in my first draft.
132. I allow myself to consciously hug and release those beliefs and fears that no longer serve me.
133. I am willing to support myself with kindness and compassion when I fall by acknowledging my feelings and my humanity.
134. I am ready to accept and integrate new lessons because each experience brings me a new perspective.
135. I am excited to be kind to myself and my words today.
136. I am excited to experience the flight and the feeling of momentum.
137. I am excited to offer myself kindness, support, and compassion and accept them from others as gifts, without expectation.
138. I trust myself to remain my own best supporter through every challenge.
139. I can't wait to welcome every new word onto the page and stay in the flow instead of jumping to correct it as it comes out.
140. I am grateful for every failure because it's teaching me to stay humble, accept my human limitations, and remain kind and compassionate to myself and others.

Now that you've read my affirmations about kindness and self-compassion, take a moment to write down three of your own. You can start with any of the following phrases that resonate with you and continue in another notebook if you feel inspired:

It's possible to…
It's safe to…
I allow myself to…
I am willing to…
I am ready to…
I am excited to…
I can't wait to…
I trust myself to…
I am grateful to…

1. _____
   _____

2. _____
   _____

3. _____
   _____

CHAPTER 15

INTEGRITY AND SELF-RESPECT

For years, I dismissed my own intuition and betrayed what mattered to me in favour of someone else's opinion. To avoid disapproval, and maybe even rejection.

Are there moments when you do the same? How does that feel?

I've done a lot of self-betrayal on my own journey. Maybe even more than most people. It started with parents and later spread to teachers, research advisors, colleagues, partners, etc. It took many years, but I finally noticed that depending on other people for acknowledgment, acceptance, and approval is exhausting. Constantly asking them to validate what we're thinking, feeling, and believing is a recipe for disaster and self-abandonment.

Yes, we're still learning. Yes, we're still figuring it out. No, we don't know for sure yet, but this is our path, and we are the ones walking it. We can still ask other people on similar journeys how they got to where they are, but we can do this with respect for the unique nature of each path, full of lessons and challenges that are custom tailored for each of us. When we respect and appreciate our own path, it becomes easier to respect and appreciate the unique paths of others.

Today, my peace comes from taking full responsibility for my choices and aligning my decisions with my own values. No matter the situation, I feel at peace because I trust myself to act with integrity and courage.

Are you ready to respect your own goals and values, without equivocation? Want to develop a new relationship with yourself so you can stop the cycle of self-betrayal and enjoy the quiet confidence that comes with integrity and self-respect? Wonderful. Repeat after me:

141. It's safe for me to let go of my need for acceptance, acknowledgement, approval, or appreciation so I can express myself in the truest way possible.
142. It's safe for me to prioritize my needs and goals and let others prioritize their own.
143. I allow myself to choose how to use my voice, my time, and my life energy.
144. I allow myself the time and space I need to consider my options so I can move forward in clarity and peace.
145. I am willing to value what I have to say.
146. I am ready to express my truth with courage and peace.
147. I am excited to look for my own clarity and truth, even if it means withdrawing for a while from the opinions of others.
148. I can't wait to see the unique truth that will be expressed through my words today.
149. I trust myself to follow the gentle guidance and light of my own heart.
150. I am grateful to be able to align my voice and my actions with my deepest values.

Now that you've read my affirmations about integrity and self-respect, take a moment to write down three of your own. You can start with any of the following phrases that resonate with you and continue in another notebook if you feel inspired:

It's possible to…
It's safe to…
I allow myself to…
I am willing to…
I am ready to…
I am excited to…
I can't wait to…
I trust myself to…
I am grateful to…

1. _____
   _____

2. _____
   _____

3. _____
   _____

CHAPTER 16

SELF-CARE AND BALANCE

What kind of relationship with ourselves do we need to develop so that we can do our best creative work? How do we take care of ourselves—our physical body, our energy levels, our focus, our mindset, and our emotions?

At first, I didn't realize that it was my responsibility and privilege to create the best possible conditions for my writing to thrive. These conditions were not limited to the external environment. They included embracing my values, needs, and priorities. I also realized that my emotional and spiritual state mattered as much as my creative goals. I had to show myself with my actions that I cared equally about the outcome and about enjoying a healthy, balanced, and sustainable writing process.

It took time and practice for me to become aware of where I was physically, emotionally, mentally, and spiritually when I came to the page. Little by little, I learned to meet myself exactly where I was and embrace my energy levels, as well as my physical and emotional needs. I learned to do the best I could with the resources I had.

If we're hungry, we can allow ourselves to take the time to prepare a snack or a meal. If we're thirsty, it's our freedom and responsibility to get up and drink a glass of water. If we are exhausted, we can close our eyes for five minutes and let them rest, while listening to an affirmation that will help us get ready to create our best work. And If our loved one needs our help, we must be able to take time away from our work guilt-free because we're clear on our values and priorities.

Are you ready to acknowledge, accept, and meet yourself exactly as you are in the moment? Are you ready to offer yourself radical care and acceptance? This is just wonderful to hear. Repeat after me:

151. It's safe to take care of my body, energy, and mindset as I write.
152. I allow myself to be present and notice what I need in order to be well and feel supported today.
153. I am willing to give equal attention and care to being productive and to my physical and mental health.
154. I am willing to pause and reset if I am experiencing an emotional, mental, or spiritual challenge.
155. I am ready to experience balance and wellness in my writing and life.
156. I am ready to acknowledge and attend to my body's needs as I'm pursuing my intellectual goals.
157. I am excited to pay close attention to my emotions as I move through my sentences and paragraphs.
158. I can't wait to prioritize my physical, mental, emotional, and spiritual wellbeing so that I can create from wellness.
159. I trust myself to give loving care to all my priorities, one at a time.
160. I trust myself to honour my body and my emotions as much as I honour my goals and results.

Now that you've read my affirmations about self-care and balance, take a moment to write down three of your own. You can start with any of the following phrases that resonate with you and continue in another notebook if you feel inspired:

It's possible to…
It's safe to…
I allow myself to…
I am willing to…
I am ready to…
I am excited to…
I can't wait to…
I trust myself to…
I am grateful to…

1. _____
   _____

2. _____
   _____

3. _____
   _____

CHAPTER 17

PLAYFULNESS

When was the last time you allowed yourself to play? To spend time daydreaming about possibilities and best-case scenarios? To move through your day and your writing without rushing or being stressed?

When I was a kid, imagination and play filled my days and my heart. I felt alive, creative, carefree, and full of energy and dreams. I effortlessly created new adventures out of the most mundane things, like chairs, fabrics, and clothespins. Did you do that too?

What happened to us? When did we decide to stop playing? And what did we replace playfulness with? I feel that many of us have replaced it with seriousness, exhaustion, and all kinds of "shoulds" and "musts." And yet, somehow, we feel that these new rules are not serving us that well.

Thank goodness that, after decades of following all the rules, I crumbled under the pressure of writing in graduate school. I got so tired of always being tense and worried if my words were good enough, that I decided I had to stop taking writing so seriously. I remembered the light and playful attitude of creating things when I was a child, and I gave myself permission to embody that essence and to play on the page. Words became blocks for building castles in my imagination.

Playing is not wasting time. Playfulness is a place for exploration, expansion, experimentation, and creativity. Writing is a process of discovery, and if we don't allow space for that, our writing will become dull and lifeless, full of other people's formulas.

Let's go back to our natural creative impulse. Let's stop being so serious about our creativity and life and see if we might enjoy both a little more.

Natalya Androsova

Want to add a bit more play to your hard work? Ready to feel the joy of integrating playfulness into your writing process? I'm so glad. Repeat after me:

161. It's safe for me to play on the page and take my playtime seriously.
162. I allow my writer within to play as I remove all pressure and expectations in her way.
163. I allow my imagination to take me places I didn't anticipate and to explore new directions in my writing.
164. I am willing to be curious and dedicated to the process of creation without being too attached to the outcome.
165. I am ready to discover what I can create by nourishing my imagination and the playful part of me.
166. I am excited to embrace my imagination and start making wonderful discoveries.
167. I am excited to follow my imagination with joyful abandon.
168. I can't wait to play with words today.
169. I trust myself to be a brave explorer and go on a fun writing adventure into the unknown.
170. I am grateful to make playfulness a big part of my creative process and trust my imagination more and more each time I write.

Now that you've read my affirmations about playfulness, take a moment to write down three of your own. You can start with any of the following phrases that resonate with you and continue in another notebook if you feel inspired:

It's possible to...
It's safe to...
I allow myself to...
I am willing to...
I am ready to...
I am excited to...
I can't wait to...
I trust myself to...
I am grateful to...

1. _____
   _____

2. _____
   _____

3. _____
   _____

CHAPTER 18

SELF-TRUST

I used to doubt myself and my words at every stage: when I drafted them, when I revised them, and when I shared them with others. Waiting for feedback was torture because my mind would automatically go to the worst-case scenario. I desperately wanted to stop obsessing about my words and other people's reactions. I wanted to untangle my worth as a writer from the feedback and enjoy the moment. I wanted to trust myself enough to be able to do my best and be content with my best effort. At some point, in the last year of my PhD, a big shift occurred and I started asking myself:

Do *you* like your words?
Do *you* think they're good enough to be shared?
Do *you* think you're good enough?

Self-trust felt truer and kinder in my nervous system, even if my mind habits were strong. All I had to do was trust myself to do my best, learn, and adapt along the way. I began to trust myself to keep taking the next small step in front of me. I began to trust myself to take care of myself and my writer within. Especially when the going got tough, and my inner critic kept chiming in. I trusted life to be my teacher throughout the entire writing journey. I'd say it worked because this is my fifth book.

How much self-trust do you feel when you're writing? Do you imagine that readers will like or hate your words? We tend to exercise our self-doubt muscle every single day, habitually, on auto-pilot. We are really good at it because we've used it so much. This self-doubt habit becomes our auto response, while our self-trust muscle is much harder to use or even to locate in the first place.

What if we looked for it, located it, and intentionally gave it the same attention and energy every day that we give our self-doubt? Let's make it a point to exercise self-trust daily, especially when challenges arise. It takes the same amount of energy to cultivate self-trust that it does to cultivate self-doubt, but the results couldn't be more different.

Want to intentionally practice self-trust instead of self-doubt every day? I'm so glad to hear. Welcome to a new relationship with yourself. Repeat after me:

171. It's safe to continue writing no matter what doubts arise.
172. It's safe to let my authenticity, my voice, and my truth guide me on this journey.
173. I allow myself to trust my gut and write as if I am the only person in the universe.
174. I am willing to safeguard my work for as long as I need before I feel safe to share and ask for feedback.
175. I am willing to lean on faith and trust in the face of each doubt.
176. I am ready to start the writing journey and trust myself to make it all the way.
177. I can't wait to become my most loyal supporter and always be there for myself in moments of challenge.
178. I trust myself to adapt as I navigate the ups and downs of the writing process.
179. I trust myself to know when my draft is safe to share.
180. I am grateful to trust life to prepare me for the next step and give me everything I need.

Now that you've read my affirmations about trusting yourself and the writing process, take a moment to write down three of your own. You can start with any of the following phrases that resonate with you and continue in another notebook if you feel inspired:

It's possible to…
It's safe to…
I allow myself to…
I am willing to…
I am ready to…
I am excited to…
I can't wait to…
I trust myself to…
I am grateful to…

1. _____
   _____

2. _____
   _____

3. _____
   _____

CHAPTER 19

THE "I AM" ANCHOR

How do you see yourself when no one is around, and you're one on one with your thoughts, feelings, self-image, and voices in your head?

I found it helpful to develop a practice that allows me to pause and become aware of the beliefs about myself that I bring to my day. For me, this has taken the shape of journaling, yoga, meditation, and long walks. Any form of stillness where we can become aware of the constant stream of images and stories running on the screen of our consciousness will do. From that place, we can gently examine our beliefs about who we are, our capacity and strength, and our inherent beauty.

When I saw myself as not smart, educated, or eloquent enough, I struggled with confidence because I depended solely on others for approval and appreciation. I didn't feel like I was enough. Naturally, my writing could not go beyond being a performance—for others to see, acknowledge, and appreciate. It couldn't be the free, playful, authentic, and joyful self-expression that I know it to be now, feeling instead like constant pressure.

Now I know myself as a writer. I write. This is what I do. This is what I am. I am a writer at the core of my being. I don't need to compare myself to anyone, and I don't need to judge my writing as good or bad. I can anchor myself in what I know and feel. And I know that I am enough for me. I've noticed that I am strong enough to get up every time I fall, dust myself off, and continue in the direction of my dreams. I know that I am creative enough to find simple strategies to overcome any challenge on my creative journey. I've noticed that most days, I am overflowing with ideas and create from a sense of fullness, wholeness, and joy. I noticed that I am here to honour myself and my creativity because it fulfills me and feeds my soul.

Let's take a moment to take stock of our beliefs and replace some of them that don't feel true anymore with more authentic ideas.

Want to bring attention to who you are when you come to the page each day? Want to return to the core of who you are and write from there? Repeat after me:

181. I am.
182. I am a writer. Period.
183. I am capable and resourceful.
184. I am resilient and strong.
185. I am creative and whole.
186. I am playful and free.
187. I am blessed with the gift of creativity and can't wait to share it and support others in discovering and sharing theirs.
188. I am creative and free to recreate myself every day.
189. I am sensitive, open, and attuned to my intuition.
190. This last one is a scary one for so many. Ready? Try saying this out loud to yourself first and then to others. You won't regret it!

    I am the author of an upcoming book on … (insert your dream topic).

Now that you've read my "I am" affirmations, take a moment to write down three of your own.

You can start with "I am" or any of the following phrases that resonate the most. If you're not ready to proclaim, "I am a writer," you can start by writing down "It's possible for me to be a writer" or "I allow myself to be a writer," etc. I don't know where you are in this continuum at the moment, but I know that soon, you'll be able to anchor yourself and your practice in the "I am":

> It's possible to…
> It's safe to…
> I allow myself to…
> I am willing to…
> I am ready to…
> I am excited to…
> I can't wait to…
> I trust myself to…
> I am grateful to…

1. _____

2. _____

3. _____

CHAPTER 20

CLARITY

Clarity is power. After experiencing confusion, mental fog, or writer's block, clarity is a gift. We can't force its arrival, but we can become more patient and discerning while we're waiting for clarity to show up. Writing helps bring clarity to my mind. When I experience moments of uncertainty and confusion, I don't judge myself or my writing. I don't stop writing either. I surrender my impatience and dive right into the messiness of ideas and keep writing until clarity emerges from the writing process itself.

What's required to invite clarity into the writing process is not speed or force. It's presence, attention, and deep listening—to both ourselves and our writing. I fully accept that not everything I write in my first draft will come from clarity, but I trust myself to notice any confusion during the revision process. I trust my power of discernment to know clear writing from writing that could use a bit more love and attention. I trust that with each revision, I will have a stronger sense of what's important and true. Thus, I remain connected with myself and simply observe my writing with presence and attention. I allow myself to experience the uncertainty and ambiguity because I know that my vision will become more clear with each new sweep of revisions. The more presence I can bring to my writing, the more clearly I will see. And if my clarity starts slipping away, I will take time to rest and reset fully.

When we learn to make choices from clarity in writing and in life, our decision making radically transforms. We make more authentic choices, aligned with our values and gifts. We make decisions that carry us to our best future, and we make them much faster and easier. Life will still bring uncertainty and ambiguity, but we can now move through challenges with lightness and confidence. We can recognize confusion or lack of clarity from a mile away. We know ourselves better. We trust our gut, and we are not negotiating our integrity with anyone at any price point. We are in love with our authentic voice. We are enjoying an adventure of a lifetime, and we don't want to miss a beat.

Wondering how to get back to clarity when feeling lost or confused? Are you ready to develop a new relationship with uncertainty and confusion as you write? Ready to boost your tolerance for the beautiful messiness of the writing process and life? Repeat after me:

191. It's safe for me to accept unclarity, ambiguity, and confusion as part of the writing process.
192. I allow myself to enjoy the writing process with or without clarity.
193. I allow myself to keep writing until I find clarity.
194. I am willing to admit to myself when I am not clear.
195. I am willing to feel confused because I always learn the most precious lessons from those moments.
196. I am excited to keep experimenting with new approaches until clarity reveals itself.
197. I am excited to look deeply into my heart in order to find clarity and authenticity.
198. I can't wait to bring more clarity to my draft with each revision.
199. I trust myself to write myself out of any stress, confusion, or overwhelm.
200. I am grateful to embrace uncertainty because experiencing it fully, without resistance, always leads me to discover a new clarity about myself and my writing process.

Now that you've read my affirmations about clarity, take a moment to write down three of your own. You can start with any of the following phrases that resonate with you and continue in another notebook if you feel inspired:

It's possible to…
It's safe to…
I allow myself to…
I am willing to…
I am ready to…
I am excited to…
I can't wait to…
I trust myself to…
I am grateful to…

1. _____
   _____

2. _____
   _____

3. _____
   _____

CHAPTER 21

FAITH

What's the connection between creativity and faith? Before we share our creations with others, we have to have faith in our words and in ourselves. If we don't have faith in ourselves, we will not be able to stand behind our words. We will doubt, question, and talk ourselves out of sharing what we have to say. But if other people are worthy of our faith and support, so are we, no?

Being shy as a kid and the youngest in my family, I had a painful habit of repeating something safe I heard adults or older children say because I didn't believe that I had anything smart or interesting to say of my own. For years, I denied myself my authentic voice for the fear of being judged, embarrassed, or misunderstood. Starting a journaling practice at thirteen helped me discover my voice and my faith in myself.

Sharing our writing and our authentic voice are both scary. It takes courage and faith. But it also helps us grow in confidence and self-trust. In the process, we also get to know what we sound like on paper and what we have to say. Through practice, we get to know our own voice, truth, and wisdom.

Want to experience what it's like to have faith in yourself and your own words? Here are a few affirmations to help you continue nourishing the flower of faith day after day. Repeat after me:

201. It is possible for me to have faith in myself and my words before anyone else does.
202. I allow myself the gift of unconditional faith.
203. I am willing to believe in my ability to create meaning and beauty in this world.
204. I am willing to be the first to support my fragile ideas and words with strong faith and gentle words of encouragement.
205. I am willing to be the last one standing and cheering myself on with a heart full of faith and kind words when no one else is there to support me.
206. I am ready to align with faith when doubts arise.
207. I am excited to have faith in myself and my writing without needing to prove my worth.
208. I can't wait to always be in my own corner (right next to Natalya).
209. I trust myself to always have faith in myself, without conditions or expectations.
210. I am grateful to stay grounded in my faith and use my authentic voice in the face of possible misunderstanding, misinterpretation, or judgment.

Now that you've read my affirmations about faith, take a moment to write down three of your own. You can start with any of the following phrases that resonate with you and continue in another notebook if you feel inspired:

It's possible to…
It's safe to…
I allow myself to…
I am willing to…
I am ready to…
I am excited to…
I can't wait to…
I trust myself to…
I am grateful to…

1. _____
   _____

2. _____
   _____

3. _____
   _____

CHAPTER 22

EMPOWERMENT

How often do you find yourself looking to others for answers, acknowledgement, approval or appreciation? What about a sense of safety or purpose? I struggled with this one a lot and still slip into this pattern sometimes, but I had to learn that this was a losing battle as no one could give me what I refused to give to myself forever.

No matter how much praise or approval we receive, we will always crave more the next time around. Especially if we don't like or have doubts about what we wrote. No matter how important our work is deemed by others, if we have lost our passion or a sense of purpose or fulfillment, we will not be able to enjoy the outcome, let alone the process.

This is self-deprivation at its finest. We deprive ourselves of joy, strength, and freedom in order to receive a fleeting sense of approval or appreciation from another person. We hide behind fancy words and sentences because we're afraid to express our truth. There is no lasting joy or empowerment in that.

Let's do everything we can today to stop the cycle of people-pleasing and connect with our deep inherent power. Let's take responsibility for our dreams and take a tiny step toward them, guided by our own heart.

Do you want to finally feel free from the opinions and approval of others? Want to stand in your own strength and make empowered choices? Then repeat after me:

211. It's safe to be honest and direct in my writing.
212. I allow myself to choose simple, clear, and powerful words to express my highest truth.
213. I am willing to experience a beginner's mind every time I don't know how to proceed and keep writing.
214. I am willing to be seen and share my heart with the world.
215. I am ready to be courageous and honour my dreams.
216. I am excited to experience discomfort, uncertainty, and doubt so that I can keep writing and discovering.
217. I can't wait to take a tiny step towards my dreams right now.
218. I trust myself to embrace all the ups and downs of my process and find the strength to carry on.
219. I trust myself to finish what I've started.
220. I trust my words to have the power to serve or positively impact at least one person.

Now that you've read my affirmations about empowerment, take a moment to write down three of your own. You can start with any of the following phrases that resonate with you and continue in another notebook if you feel inspired:

It's possible to…
It's safe to…
I allow myself to…
I am willing to…
I am ready to…
I am excited to…
I can't wait to…
I trust myself to…
I am grateful to…

1. _____

2. _____

3. _____

CHAPTER 23

FREEDOM

What's in the way of your freedom when you write? Who makes decisions about what ideas to explore or how to tell your story?

Strangely enough, experiencing too much freedom might feel uncomfortable at first, but this freedom is worth exploring. It's inviting us to use our agency and intuition. We are so used to listening to other people's opinions that we must develop and practice the habit of listening to ourselves when it matters.

I still struggle with this habit at times. But I am also feeling more and more grateful for my freedom. It is both empowering and sobering to realize that it's completely up to me how I want to engage with the page, my ideas, and how I want to express my creativity. These days, I am putting fewer and fewer expectations on my words because I'm not interested in perfection. I am interested in freedom and joy, which my pen and a blank page allow me.

A page has become the playground for my spirit to learn more about itself and its mission here. I am excited to leap into the unknown, allowing my creative flow to carry me through all the obstacles and letting my spirit soar while my inner critic keeps doubting me and my writing somewhere in the distance.

Writing teaches me everything I need to know about freedom. I notice all the obstacles I create and turn them into lessons so I can move past them and become more open and free. Writing also frees me from all ideas about myself. I can take off the heavy backpack of self-images and put it down for a bit. Writing allows me to reinvent myself and make a fresh start on every new page. I can create and recreate worlds, myself, and my life. All through the magic of writing.

Writing is freedom in action. It is the movement of my soul writing my life on the blank page of time. Each day is a new page. And so is each moment.

Want to experience complete creative freedom when you write? Repeat after me:

221. I allow myself to soar in the face of uncertainty and self-doubt.
222. I allow myself to take this journey toward myself via the blank page.
223. I allow myself to cut any part of my draft during a revision if it doesn't feel right.
224. I am ready to set my writing free from all the unrealistic expectations I've put on it.
225. I am excited to explore any question, feeling, idea, or image I choose.
226. I can't wait to choose any metaphor in the world around me and give it a unique personal meaning.
227. I trust myself to play freely in my imagination without any rules or expectations.
228. I am grateful for the freedom I feel every time I come to the page.
229. I am grateful for the freedom to create anything I want.
230. I am grateful to enjoy the freedom and the magic of the creative process.

Now that you've read my affirmations about writing freedom, take a moment to write down three of your own. You can start with any of the following phrases that resonate with you and continue in another notebook if you feel inspired:

It's possible to…
It's safe to…
I allow myself to…
I am willing to…
I am ready to…
I am excited to…
I can't wait to…
I trust myself to…
I am grateful to…

1. _____
   _____

2. _____
   _____

3. _____
   _____

CHAPTER 24

WHOLENESS

Do you write from a sense of wholeness? Do you allow every part of yourself to have a voice in your writing?

If you're anything like me, you might feel uncomfortable sharing all of yourself. For so long, we were conditioned to hide. So we choose which parts of ourselves are acceptable and allowed to be expressed in our writing and which ones should be kept behind locked doors. We introduce restrictions and barriers. We keep hiding parts of ourselves from ourselves and others, trying to match our words to the image we want to have of ourselves. This approach may succeed for a while. Until writing becomes this tight and narrow space where our spirit feels suffocated.

At some point, I got tired of hiding from myself. As an artistic soul, I became deeply curious about my own secrets. I knew they had unique strengths and gifts to offer me if I finally gave them a voice. I knew that even if I never shared those parts with others, I wanted to meet the part of me hidden behind locked doors. I wanted to meet all the parts that were banned from expressing themselves in my life. I wanted to discover all parts of myself without judging them good or bad, acceptable or unacceptable. I wanted to be whole.

While we don't need to express each and every part of ourselves on the page, there is wisdom in noticing which parts we feel too scared to express. They also hold truth and wisdom. They also want to come out and play. They hold a key to our wholeness.

I still love discovering unexpected parts of myself in the sacred and safe space of the blank page. As I go on this self-discovery journey, I trust myself to stay grounded in self-love and acceptance. I hold all of myself in love and appreciation, so I can learn to hold others in true love and appreciation as well.

Want to write from a sense of wholeness? Want to feel free to express any part of you if you want to? It might feel scary, but it's worth it. Repeat after me:

231. It's safe to express myself authentically.
232. It's safe to acknowledge parts of myself that were excluded, shamed, or rejected.
233. I am willing to hear out all parts of myself that want to express themselves.
234. I am willing to suspend my judgement so that I can meet all parts of myself in a safe and sacred space of writing.
235. I am ready to meet parts of myself that were denied expression in the past and start writing from wholeness.
236. I am ready to welcome the gifts and strengths of my previously disowned parts.
237. I am excited to go on a journaling date with myself and get to know deeper, secret aspects of myself.
238. I am excited to stop shaming and rejecting parts of myself that were judged by others.
239. I can't wait to open all the doors and windows of my soul so that I can air out the stale air and let the fresh air in.
240. I am grateful to welcome my whole self on the page with curiosity, humility, and acceptance.

Now that you've read my affirmations about wholeness, take a moment to write down three of your own. You can start with any of the following phrases that resonate with you and continue in another notebook if you feel inspired:

It's possible to…
It's safe to…
I allow myself to…
I am willing to…
I am ready to…
I am excited to…
I can't wait to…
I trust myself to…
I am grateful to…

1. _____

2. _____

3. _____

CHAPTER 25

INTUITION

Do you trust your intuition? Do you sometimes get inexplicable nudges to go in a certain direction or to stay away from another?

It took me some time to learn that I could trust these nudges and hunches. Initially I was afraid of going crazy if I started listening to the voices in my head. That was before I learned to discern between the loving and gentle voice of my intuition and the voice of my mind and its loyal servant—the inner critic. There is a difference of tone and energy between the two. Oh, and volume!

Our inner critic welcomes any opportunity to scream at us, berate and shame us, and make us doubt our worth or goodness. Ouch! Let's not trust that one again.

But we can trust the quiet voice of our intuition because it comes directly from our loving heart. It speaks softly and shows us the way of peace and kindness. It knows the answers to all our questions, even before we are able to formulate them.

When my mind wants me to speed up and panic in the face of new challenges, I do the opposite. I slow down and sit quietly until a solution emerges and clarity returns.

Want to experience the incredible power of intuition? Want to grow in discernment so you never confuse the voice of your intuition with the voice of your inner critic? I'm happy to hear this. Repeat after me:

241. It is safe for me to trust the voice of my own heart.
242. It's safe for me to trust the voice of my heart because it only offers peace, patience, and wisdom in any situation.
243. I allow myself to trust my loving heart because it's been trustworthy.
244. I am willing to trust my intuition when the mind is trying to scare me with worst-case scenarios.
245. I am ready to practice following my intuition so I can grow in discernment and trust.
246. I am excited to trust my intuition more than the voice of my mind, my inner critic, and my self-doubt.
247. I trust myself to know when my writing doesn't sound right.
248. I can't wait to see my intuition grow stronger.
249. I trust my heart to know the answers to all my questions.
250. I am grateful to trust my heart from now on.

Now that you've read my affirmations about intuition, take a moment to write down three of your own. You can start with any of the following phrases that resonate with you and continue in another notebook if you feel inspired:

It's possible to…
It's safe to…
I allow myself to…
I am willing to…
I am ready to…
I am excited to…
I can't wait to…
I trust myself to…
I am grateful to…

1. _____
   _____

2. _____
   _____

3. _____
   _____

CHAPTER 26

DREAMS

Do you tend to focus more on possibilities or limitations? Do you intentionally spend some time every week dreaming about the best possible scenarios? Would you like to?

Dreaming big and cultivating a sense of wonder are not what I was taught in school. I was conditioned to follow the rules, be aware of potential risks and dangers, and avoid any traps. I learned to play it safe and stay in my comfort zone. Until I ran out of air.

Our teachers and parents have the best intentions—to protect us and keep us safe. What's sad is when staying safe impacts our ability to dream big. What if everything turns out even better than we'd imagined? What if a miraculous synchronicity shows up and clears our path of all self-imposed limitations?

Can we allow ourselves to dream big and imagine best-case scenarios? Can we allow ourselves to feel worthy of life's best gifts and start seeing possibilities everywhere, like we did when we were children? I gave myself permission to dream of writing, publishing, and helping others through my coaching. I also gave myself permission to leave my great full-time job in the name of my greater dreams. And it worked out.

I love to spend time daydreaming about the best-case scenarios for myself and my writing, and I support these scenarios by visualizing them in detail, feeling into them, and breathing faith into them. I don't hold on too tightly to my vision. I play. I create my dreams, savour them, hug them for a moment, and let them fly free. I simply stay open to and anticipate all the incredible opportunities and synchronicities that are coming my way.

Want to restore a sense of dreaming and seeing possibilities everywhere? I'm happy to get you started with a few permissions, so that you can continue building your own repertoire from here on. Repeat after me:

251. It's safe to dream.
252. I am willing to dream bigger than before.
253. I am ready to put in the work and be open to synchronicities, guidance, and miracles.
254. I am ready to accept new invitations and walk through opening doors with full trust.
255. I am excited to discover what could turn out well today.
256. I am excited to be on the lookout for good signs of things to come.
257. I trust myself to set aside time each week to intentionally dream of miraculous possibilities.
258. I can't wait to dream again in my writing and life.
259. I can't wait to see my dreams come true!
260. I am grateful to be in awe of life's magical orchestration.

Now that you've read my affirmations about dreams, take a moment to write down three of your own. You can start with any of the following phrases that resonate with you and continue in another notebook if you feel inspired:

It's possible to…
It's safe to…
I allow myself to…
I am willing to…
I am ready to…
I am excited to…
I can't wait to…
I trust myself to…
I am grateful to…

1. _____

2. _____

3. _____

CHAPTER 27

CONNECTION

What are you connected to when you write?

It might not be a conscious connection, but if we stop to look, we might be surprised to discover that we're connected to something we didn't consciously choose. Once we see it, we can disconnect from it and choose more intentionally. That's the power of awareness.

For example, we may discover that we're connected to our inner critic, our logical brain, our old fears, or a sense of lack. We might be writing while connected to stress, anxiety, a sense of obligation, or a childhood trauma that makes us feel that we're not good enough, no matter what we accomplish.

It is much better if we take a moment to consciously connect to our sense of purpose, vision, and values. We can also connect to our sense of shared humanity that allows us to relate to every human being on the planet. We might also choose to connect with those writers who have been our role models and inspired us to pick up a pen in the first place.

For me, writing is my connection with myself, my spirit, my community, my ancestors, and my future that is calling me to create from the most honest and authentic life. And I gratefully accept this responsibility and honour this call by connecting to my dreams every time I come to the page.

What or whom do you want to connect to? What energy do you choose to be a part of your writing process? Let's take a moment to support our process by choosing our connection consciously. Repeat after me:

261. It's safe for me to connect with my higher purpose before I write a word.
262. I allow myself to connect with all the writers who have touched my soul with their words and inspired me to start writing.
263. I am willing to connect to my biggest dreams as I write today.
264. I am willing to connect with the sense of joy of walking in the direction of my dreams.
265. I am ready to connect with my unique gifts and strengths and share them through my writing.
266. I am excited to connect with other creatives who dare to dream big and change the world through their creativity.
267. I am excited to connect with my future self who has achieved the dreams I've cherished since I was a little girl.
268. I am excited to connect with my writer within and create my most honest, powerful, and courageous writing yet.
269. I trust myself to connect to my loving heart.
270. I am grateful to be connected to my community and feel supported by our shared dreams and values.

Now that you've read my affirmations about connection, take a moment to write down three of your own. You can start with any of the following phrases that resonate with you and continue in another notebook if you feel inspired:

It's possible to…
It's safe to…
I allow myself to…
I am willing to…
I am ready to…
I am excited to…
I can't wait to…
I trust myself to…
I am grateful to…

1. _____
   _____

2. _____
   _____

3. _____
   _____

CHAPTER 28

RESPONSIBILITY

What is our responsibility to ourselves and others? Are we responsible for making other people feel good, or are we responsible to ourselves and our heart for aligning our words and actions with our dreams and values? Who is responsible for our happiness and peace, and for the calling inside our heart?

It may seem counterintuitive, but taking responsibility for my decisions and actions was the door to ultimate freedom for me. It was a complete inversion of my perspective, especially because I had a habit of blaming my circumstances or other people for the lack of options or positive outcomes I encountered. It still shows up sometimes.

When I am able to shift my attention from making excuses to taking full responsibility for my choices, I feel unstoppable. I feel eager to keep walking toward my dreams and can see new options and possibilities that were not visible to me before. I love the responsibility and freedom of making my own creative choices and being my own cheerleader as I'm moving towards my goals.

It even feels exciting to take responsibility for making mistakes, because how else would I be able to practice discernment and grow in confidence and self-trust? I am not after perfection. My heart is set on freedom. Nothing less will do.

Want to take responsibility for your creativity and your life? What are you ready to take responsibility for in this moment? May these words inspire you to look deeper and find your own precise and powerful words. Repeat after me:

271. It's safe to take responsibility for all my creative decisions.
272. I allow myself to use my courage and intuition to choose the best way forward.
273. I am willing to take responsibility for building a healthy, sustainable, and joyful writing practice.
274. I am willing to take responsibility for my happiness and self-expression.
275. I am ready to make my own creative choices and take full responsibility for each one.
276. I am ready to take responsibility for providing the best conditions for my writer within to thrive and create freely.
277. I am excited to imagine, explore, and implement my creative ideas.
278. I am excited to make all my creative decisions by myself, freely and playfully, and to keep moving forward with lightness and ease.
279. I trust myself to discern when to encourage myself to keep going and when to allow time for rest and recovery.
280. I trust myself to show up on the page in an authentic and vulnerable way.

Now that you've read my affirmations about responsibility, take a moment to write down three of your own. You can start with any of the following phrases that resonate with you and continue in another notebook if you feel inspired:

It's possible to…
It's safe to…
I allow myself to…
I am willing to…
I am ready to…
I am excited to…
I can't wait to…
I trust myself to…
I am grateful to…

1. _____

2. _____

3. _____

CHAPTER 29

COMMUNITY

You are strong, resilient, creative, and smart. No doubt about that. But can you really complete this journey alone? Me neither. No need to do this solo. We are so much stronger when we walk together, and our nervous systems instantly relax when we know that we're not alone.

I've always found strength in surrounding myself with a supportive community of practice, so that we can encourage and support each other, especially when we stumble or fall. It takes courage to open up to others about your struggle and ask for support. It can be really hard, especially if we've been conditioned to excel, compete, and overachieve. It's common to experience this sense of competitiveness in school, for instance. And if you also went to graduate school, chances are, your instinct to isolate yourself and keep your struggles to yourself got even stronger.

How often do you wish you had someone to talk to when you've hit a snag in your writing process? Do you feel comfortable opening up about your struggles and asking for support? Do you feel open to joining or building a community?

Imposter syndrome is a very isolating condition of doubting ourselves and our writing. I suffered from it for a long time. It's a secret belief that our work is not good and we don't deserve to be "here," wherever that is for each of us. It's a nagging suspicion that any success we had was a fluke and that at some point we will get found out and be rejected as a fraud by our community. Almost every writer feels this way at one point or another. It leads to loneliness and fear instead of an authentic connection with other writers like ourselves.

Our beliefs about ourselves can either support or sabotage our ability to join or build a community. But we have the power to choose the right beliefs to follow. Though it can take courage to open up to others, we can learn to cultivate a sense of safety and trust within our writing communities. I cherish my community and am excited to strengthen it with my trust, encouragement, and an unwavering support of others. We are here to support each other on this brave creative journey.

Natalya Androsova

Are you ready to enjoy a relationship with your community, so that you can appreciate, amplify, and be nourished by the power of the beautiful humans around you? Repeat after me:

281. It's possible for me to open up to others about my struggles, obstacles, and setbacks and ask for support.
282. It's safe to share my work and my process with others so that we can connect, learn, and grow together.
283. I allow myself to reach out to others in order to join a community of practice or build one.
284. I am willing to ask for guidance and support when I feel lost, confused, or overwhelmed.
285. I am ready to open myself up to building or joining a community of support and accountability.
286. I am excited to recognize and embrace the opportunities to join others.
287. I can't wait to support others on this creative journey with generosity and grace.
288. I trust myself to be there for myself and others and to offer warm, gentle, and kind words of encouragement and support.
289. I am grateful for every genuine and authentic connection on the journey.
290. I am grateful for the beauty of a community of support and accountability.

Now that you've read my affirmations about community, take a moment to write down three of your own. You can start with any of the following phrases that resonate with you and continue in another notebook if you feel inspired:

It's possible to…
It's safe to…
I allow myself to…
I am willing to…
I am ready to…
I am excited to…
I can't wait to…
I trust myself to…
I am grateful to…

1. _____

2. _____
   _____

3. _____
   _____

CHAPTER 30

COMMITMENT

Like any craft, writing requires a serious commitment and dedication. I fell in love with writing thirty-seven years ago and haven't had a change of heart yet.

Through all the ups and downs, through all the trials and tribulations, through every crisis, loss, and confusion, I've remained faithful to the practice I love. You may call it discipline, but I call it love. I also call it devotion. I am a disciple of writing and come to its temple every day. Each day, I bring my open heart to the blank page and start learning all over again, as if for the first time.

After almost four decades of practice, what stands out as the most important ingredient is an unwavering commitment to come to the page and to start. Consistently, each day. Without hiding behind excuses and without conditions. It's a commitment to the process, to the wisdom of practice, to listening to my heart. It's also a commitment to myself. A permission slip to stay loyal to what I love and to continue learning from it every day.

I trust the flow of the writing process more than I trust the rigidity of my mind. And I strengthen this trust by showing up every day. I am grateful to have been in love with writing for so long and am committed to sharing my love with others and helping them fall in love with writing as well.

What commitments are you honouring when you write?

Are you ready to explore your commitments and connect with your why? What do you love and are ready to commit to? What will you stay loyal to, no matter what? Repeat after me:

291. I allow the writing process to teach me what I need to know.
292. I allow myself to stay madly in love with writing and dedicate my life to loving it.
293. I am willing to keep writing in the face of any obstacles.
294. I am willing to show up consistently every day, no matter the circumstances.
295. I am ready to keep my promise to myself so that my writing muscle and my confidence can grow.
296. I am excited to surrender to the wisdom of the craft so that I can keep enjoying learning from it.
297. I am excited to honour my unique way of writing, thinking, and being in the world through my practice.
298. I can't wait to be there for myself in moments of doubt and confusion and lean on my love of writing to get back to clarity and self-trust.
299. I can't wait to continue this life-long friendship with writing and to find new ways to show my commitment, loyalty, and dedication to this beautiful art and way of being.
300. I trust myself to stay loyal to my love of writing, no matter what.

Now that you've read my affirmations about commitment, take a moment to write down three of your own. You can start with any of the following phrases that resonate with you and continue in another notebook if you feel inspired:

It's possible to…
It's safe to…
I allow myself to…
I am willing to…
I am ready to…
I am excited to…
I can't wait to…
I trust myself to…
I am grateful to…

1. _____

_____

2. _____

_____

3. _____

_____

CHAPTER 31

WONDER

Do we really need to know everything about the next step, page, or stage of our project? Do we only allow ourselves to move forward when we feel completely safe? Do we always need guarantees before taking the next step? Or do we dare to approach life as an unfolding mystery and stand there wide-eyed and open-hearted in awe and wonder like we used to when we were children?

I've discovered that there is so much richness, nuance, complexity, paradox, and beauty to be found in places that inspire in me a childlike sense of wonder. I love to find those places and feel small before the mystery of the universe. I love being with the mystery, going deeper into it, and exploring unexpected directions for my writing and life. I intentionally open myself up to an almost irresistible pull to take the leap into the great unknown. And whenever I feel the pressure to know the answer, I simply surrender it and keep choosing a sense of awe and wonder over and over again.

From that place, in that moment of feeling awestruck and mesmerized by the beauty and mystery of it all, I have been able to discover the most interesting questions that have no answers but radiate infinite power. From that place, I can take a step forward and balance on the edge of mystery. I trust myself to keep my balance. From there, I can invite my reader to come along with me into the heart of adventure.

Are you ready to stand in awe and wonder on the edge of mystery? Great! Let's discover our courage and strength that are gifts of this openness. Repeat after me:

301. It's safe to move forward without knowing how.
302. I allow myself to take the next small step, guided only by a sense of openness, curiosity, and trust.
303. I am willing to follow my sense of awe and wonder into uncharted territory.
304. I am ready to savour a sense of awe and wonder as part of learning and discovery.
305. I am excited to discover deep, genuine questions even if I don't have any answers yet.
306. I can't wait to discover new questions that take me beyond what I already know.
307. I can't wait to explore new secret areas of knowledge.
308. I trust myself to remain loyal to a sense of wonder as I write and live.
309. I trust myself to ask questions from a place of openness and not knowing.
310. I am grateful to remain an apprentice of writing who is open to learning and growth.

Now that you've read my affirmations about a sense of wonder, take a moment to write down three of your own. You can start with any of the following phrases that resonate with you and continue in another notebook if you feel inspired:

It's possible to…
It's safe to…
I allow myself to…
I am willing to…
I am ready to…
I am excited to…
I can't wait to…
I trust myself to…
I am grateful to…

1. _____

_____

2. _____

_____

3. _____

_____

CHAPTER 32

SPIRITUALITY

Writing has been more than a personal and professional practice for me. It has been a lifelong spiritual practice that allows me to explore life's deepest questions. In that way, writing has been my teacher of wisdom and light, my master and my guru. I didn't ask for it to happen this way, but I can recognize and acknowledge its role in my life over the past three and a half decades.

Writing has taught me many lessons about life, courage, freedom, and love. It has set me free from many limiting beliefs about myself, because beliefs we hold about writing are not different from the beliefs we hold about ourselves and the world. For example, if I feel my writing is not good enough, I probably think that I am not good enough either. If I strive for perfection in my writing, then I probably demand perfection from myself and my life. If I hold an "all or nothing" belief about my draft, I will apply the same belief to myself and the world. When I am able to see through these limiting beliefs about my writing, they release their hold in all other areas of my life.

I have full trust in writing as my greatest teacher in life. I recognize and fully accept its connection to the spirit. And even if the lessons are too deep for me to understand completely right away, I remain open to discovering more and more about myself and life through my writing practice.

Do you feel curious about exploring a spiritual dimension of your writing practice? Are you enjoying a strong relationship with your spirituality, or do you feel like inviting more of it into your creative endeavours?

Each person's path is unique, so, as always, your personal affirmations will mean more than mine. I'm glad that by this spot in the book, you've practiced creating a lot of them and can use your skills to craft words that will fill your practice with an even deeper meaning.

But let me share with you some of mine. I hope they serve you, too. Repeat after me and see which ones resonate with you, and expand on those by creating your own:

311. It's safe to explore a deeper connection between writing and spirituality.
312. I allow myself to look for a deeper meaning behind my desire to create.
313. I allow myself to see my writing as a spiritual practice connected to the deeper meaning of life.
314. I am willing to explore the deeper meaning of creativity in my life.
315. I am ready to discover the deeper needs writing serves in my life and the deeper questions it's helping me answer.
316. I am excited to embrace the spiritual dimension of writing with its lessons, gifts, and insights.
317. I can't wait to discover a deeper spiritual meaning in all my creative endeavours.
318. I trust my writing practice to continue expanding my awareness.
319. I trust my writing to keep lifting the internal and external veils and help me continue to increase my awareness.
320. I am grateful for the way spirituality enriches my writing and my life.

Now that you've read my affirmations about spirituality, take a moment to write down three of your own. You can start with any of the following phrases that resonate with you and continue in another notebook if you feel inspired:

It's possible to…
It's safe to…
I allow myself to…
I am willing to…
I am ready to…
I am excited to…
I can't wait to…
I trust myself to…
I am grateful to…

1. _____

2. _____

3. _____

CHAPTER 33

GRATITUDE

Does gratitude feature prominently in your writing practice? It's at the core of mine.

I am grateful for my love of writing. This love has allowed me to persevere through the ups and downs of the creative process and to express my depth and truth. It has given me the gifts of connection and belonging to the tribe of the most incredible writers, past and present.

I am deeply grateful for my creative calling. I love the sense of playfulness that allows me to discover new ideas and new ways of expressing myself. I am grateful for this magical journey that writing took me on. Each time I take a step into the unknown, a path opens up in front of me. I am grateful for this most unusual guidance and navigation system.

All that's required is the trust and the willingness to take the first step, in spite of the many fears we have, and I had more than most. Yes, it takes courage and strength to be seen, but gratitude has an incredible power to take us from a state of stress and anxiety to a calm and centered state, in which we can notice and appreciate the strength we already have.

Gratitude is a radical approach to writing and wellness. It only takes a few moments to refocus our attention and energy from lack to abundance, and we can start appreciating dozens of little things we don't usually notice, but that, nonetheless, add meaning, beauty, and joy to our day.

Want to harness the incredible power of gratitude? I can help you get started with a few affirmations, so that you can continue building your gratitude list and filling your heart with appreciation and enjoyment every day for the rest of your life. Repeat after me:

321. I am grateful for my creativity.
322. I am grateful for my inner critic because it helps me discover my true values, resilience, and strength.
323. I am grateful for the courage to share my truth and vision with others.
324. I am grateful for the courage to share myself with others in humility and vulnerability.
325. I am grateful for my love of writing.
326. I am grateful for every challenge because it allows me to grow stronger and look deeper.
327. I am grateful for my dreams because they take me to places I could never imagine.
328. I am grateful for my self-doubt because it shows me when I need to learn to trust myself.
329. I am grateful for my self-trust because it gave me joy and strength that self-doubt could never give.
330. I am grateful for my willingness to dream, play, and create.

Now that you've read my affirmations about gratitude, take a moment to write down three of your own. You can start with any of the following phrases that resonate with you and continue in another notebook if you feel inspired:

I am grateful to…
I am grateful for…
I am grateful that…

1. _____

_____

2. _____

_____

3. _____

_____

The Last Three Permission Slips

If you've reached this point in the book, congratulations and repeat after me one last time:

331. It's safe for me to ignore anything in this book that doesn't resonate with me and to create my own permission slips that support my unique practice.
332. I trust myself to take what I need from this book in order to create a beautiful, inspiring, and healthy practice.
333. I can't wait to support my writing dreams by nourishing my writer within.

Now that you've read all of my 333 affirmations, take a moment to write down three of your own. You can start with any of the following phrases that resonate with you and continue in another notebook if you feel inspired:

It's possible to…
It's safe to…
I allow myself to…
I am willing to…
I am ready to…
I am excited to…
I can't wait to…
I trust myself to…
I am grateful to…

1. _____
   _____

2. _____
   _____

3. _____
   _____

THREE SPECIAL BONUSES

BONUS ONE

Five Love Notes

Love Note to My Writer Within

Dear Writer Within,

Thank you for being here all these years.

I am sorry that I have been neglecting your voice until today.

From now on, I promise to listen to you, even if I feel scared or uncomfortable hearing what you have to say.

Please share with me what you have always wanted to express and ask for anything you need. I promise to listen and take your words to heart. I will try to give you what you need whenever I can.

With love,
Natalya

Writing Challenge

Copy the above note and hand sign your name at the end. Then read it out loud, and write down what your writer within has to say in response. Keep writing without stopping for at least five minutes.

Do the same with the other four notes that follow, handwriting and formatting them like an actual letter, and writing a response from the one you're addressing in each note.

Love Note to My Inner Critic

Dear Inner Critic,

Thank you for trying to protect me from failure and embarrassment. I appreciate you and your desire to help, but please know that what you have to give is no longer needed here. I am good. Thank you for your help and service. You can rest now.

With love,
Natalya

Love Note to Fear and Anxiety

Dear Fear and Anxiety,

Thank you for trying to protect me from every possible "what if" scenario. I deeply appreciate your care but have to decline your services because I now have trust in my ability to tolerate uncertainty.

With love,
Natalya

Love Note to My Inner Perfectionist

Dear Inner Perfectionist,

Thank you for trying to help me write the best possible drafts, sentences, and paragraphs. Please know that you can rest now because I no longer need to produce perfect drafts or sentences. I prefer the joy and flow of writing to striving for perfection.

With love,
Natalya

Love Note to Myself

Dear Self,

Thank you for waking up to the joy of writing and for choosing to nourish your relationship with the writer within and for letting go of the one with the inner critic. I am proud of you and love the way you trust yourself these days.

With love,
Natalya

BONUS TWO

Renewing My Vows to My Writer Within

1. I promise to listen to you and protect you from my inner critic's attacks.
2. I promise to create a safe space for you to share what you've always wanted to share.
3. I promise to cherish our relationship and support you every step of the way.
4. I promise to support you with everything I have if you're experiencing a challenge.
5. I promise to create regular time and space for us to get together, play, and explore our wildest ideas.
6. I promise to ask for support and guidance when I feel stuck.
7. I promise to choose you over my inner critic every single time.
8. I promise to return to you and our work every time my inner critic manages to steal my attention for a bit.
9. I promise to keep our sacred time together distraction free.
10. I promise to honour my commitment to you and to myself.

Writing Challenge

Have you ever created writer's vows? This might be a good moment for you to create or renew your vows. You can start by reading mine out loud and then write down your own vows to yourself, your writing, or your writer within. Try to create at least ten. You might be surprised by what you come up with.

Best of luck! You've got this.

BONUS THREE

Fifteen Questions to Support Your Writing Process

1. What will it take for me to reach my writing dreams?
2. What will it take for me to reach my goals while remaining kind to myself and my writing?
3. What support structure could I create?
4. What systems could I put into place?
5. Whom can I ask for support right now?
6. What is the best way I can support myself right now?
7. What if I remove all pressure from my writing process for the next 30 minutes?
8. What if I detach myself from the outcome and focus on the joy of creative expression?
9. What if it works out better than expected?
10. What is the worst that could happen? What will I do if it does?
11. What is the best that could happen? What will I do if it does?
12. What am I ready for in this moment?
13. What tiny step am I willing to take right now?
14. What courageous decision will I make today?
15. What small action can I take right now to help me move forward?

As you're building your own confidence in yourself, you can borrow mine. You've got this!

Writing Challenge

Feel into your current writer's block. Try asking yourself at least 10 questions about it, knowing that you don't have to answer them if you don't want to. Just look for new ways to see what's blocking you.

You might be surprised by what you discover by simply asking meaningful questions. And if you really feel like it, freewrite for a few minutes in response to any of your own questions.

Best of luck! You've got this.

A Note From the Author

Thank you for reading this book. Creating a genuine connection with readers like you is why I wrote it. Thank you for your trust and for giving these permissions a try. I hope they serve you as well as they served me. If after you've tried these, you have any feedback or questions, I'd love to hear from you. Feel free to email me directly at natalya@writingdissertationcoach.com

If you enjoyed the book, I'd appreciate a rating or a short review on Amazon or Goodreads. For an indie author, every review is a precious gift.

If you've been struggling with your inner critic or writer's block, you can download FREE chapters from my books at www.writingdissertationcoach.com/free

There you'll also find FREE writing meditations that will help you build a simple and effective daily practice.

For unique coaching programs, writing groups, and retreats, visit www.writingdissertationcoach.com

And when you're ready to break up with your inner critic and trade anxiety for clarity, momentum, and joy, reach out and book a FREE call with me.

Let's make your writing dreams a reality.

www.ingramcontent.com/pod-product-compliance
Lightning Source LLC
Chambersburg PA
CBHW071850070526
44583CB00016B/1616